C000015511

LIFE'S RICH PATTERN

A collection of poems by

Adrienne Winter

Preface

These poems are collected thoughts about life and faith, gathered over many years. I have put them together with some of my paintings, and hope they may enhance your puzzling too.

This book is dedicated to my dear friends and family, with special thanks for help to John Webster and Wendy Allen.

AW

Copyright © Adrienne Winter 2020
First published 2020 by

ISBN: 978-1-914002-00-7

The right of Adrienne Winter to be identified as the Author of this Work
has been asserted by her in accordance with the
Copyright, Designs and Patents Act 1988.

All rights reserved. No part of this publication may be reproduced, stored in a
retrieval system, or transmitted, in any form or by any means, electronic,
mechanical, photocopying, recording or otherwise, without the prior permission
of the publisher or a licence permitting restricted copying. In the UK such
licences are issued by the Copyright Licensing Agency,
90 Tottenham Court Road, London W1P 9HE.

Further copies of this book, as well as details of other publications and services,
are available from: www.wordsbydesign.co.uk

Contents

ΡΙΔΔΛΕ

Τηε μονκεψ–πυζζλε τρεε

Φελλ δοων ιν α λιγητ ωινδ τηε οτηερ δαψ.

"Τηε συπερφιχιαλ σοιλ

Ωασ φαρ τοο ριχη φορ ιτ"

Τηε φαρμερ σαιδ.

"Ι σηουλδ ηαϖε κεπτ τηε χοωσ ανδ σηεεπ αωαψ

Ορ πρυνεδ ιτσ ροοτσ το μακε τηεμ γο δοων δεεπ."

Ι τηουγητ : "Τηατ ισ

Α ριδδλε φορ α μαν."

RIDDLE

The monkey-puzzle tree

Fell down in a light wind the other day.

"The superficial soil

Was far too rich for it"

The farmer said.

"I should have kept the cows and sheep away

Or pruned its roots to make them go down deep."

I thought : "That is a riddle for a man."

Headship

In the world around

Leadership is rank

And pride of place holds sway.

His is another way –

Example, service.

Woman out of man was made,

Created order there displayed.

It's harder if we take the lead ourselves,

Take over, and remove from men we love

That God-intended final impetus,

Decision's consequence,

To drive them to his arms,

Where only, they can learn

To lead indeed.

Bargain

'Take me as I am, or not at all!'
"Most gladly, for the price that I recall"

'Leave me as I am, or I'll not come.'
"Ah, that I cannot do for any sum."

'Well, make some small adjustments here and there!'
"No, that would never do for one so fair."

'Then take me on for change and growth and gain!'
"That shall be done, by love and truth and pain."

'Now tell me how much still remains to pay?'
"I met the cost in full, one blood-rent day."

'What kind of trade is this – unequal, strange?
You pay the price, and I keep all the change.'

Rescue-work

You can't make an ark overnight.

The dark

is not an easy time to build,

and a complexity of trust

is not just willed.

Arc-light

is blinding to work by.

So build before sunset

and let

the fabric be sound;

planks caulked with obedience,

difficult feelings talked through

and resolved;

hearts pitched together

in God's will.

Cries

When someone cries:

"Hold me safe!"

"Get me out!"

"Rescue me!"

"Show me the truth!"

"Help me grow!"

"Dress my wounds!"

"Forgive!"

"I'm famished, thirsty,

Terror-struck!"

A scream, a groan, a sigh

or just

The feeble trickle of a tear,

Tears at his heart

because

His name's invoked.

And he who loves

will come.

Painful Fence

The fence you're sitting on is topped with spikes.
This is your future if you do not choose to
Change:
Crisis on crisis;
Disillusionments;
Vain hopes shattered;
Bruises and injuries;
Being the doll used
In vile adulteries and things much worse
(But you are not a doll,
Precious life-spirit
Born of God in temple-body);
Being corruption's means
For other beings meant for heaven too;
Doss-houses, needles, crime;
Heroin-with-debt your one hell-forked relief,
Suicide thoughts and plans, woven with fear,
And then enacted.
But you *can* choose to
>Change;
>To grasp the proffered hand;
>To count the cost as nothing,
>And already paid for you;
>To leave this life behind in watery grave
>-Another way of death,
>-A way of freedom and of future hope.
One day you will,
And only you will know when that day comes,
And mark it not by promises, but
Actions.

HOME ALONE

The bolts are shot, the shutters tight.
I sit despairing here,
Exhausted by the ceaseless drudge of work
(All I have ever known)
Drained of all tears,
Hugging my hatred,
Weary of keeping all the cupboard doors
Pushed shut,
So that no thought of what's inside should overwhelm me –
Make me less efficient –
Threaten my job (my only end in life).
Easiest to hate secretly,
Bottle the anger like an alcoholic
(There it is again – a twist of piercing pain).
No-one shall share my agony.
Why should they want to?
I'm on my own just as I've always been,
Stuffing my face to fill the aching void,
Alone, rejected and abandoned.
Love is a disappointing dream, not real.
TV and wireless block out the silence
Quite satisfactorily.
No troublesome whispers from the past
Can sidle through that way.
The future lies unthinkably ahead –
More of the same, or else quite cataclysmic.

What is that ceaseless knocking at the door?
I wish they'd stop – it's giving me a headache.

Dancing the Changes

Changing relationships and rôles in life
Is like a complex dance which must be learned:
New steps
And weaving turns
With linking and unlinking to and fro,
Announced by weddings, funerals or births.
Toes trodden on, skirts torn and faces red
Are not a sign of failure, but of growth
In gracefulness –
Part of the vital process –
Copying, faltering, gaining confidence,
Until at last ease comes with practised skill:
Son is a father, husband, son-in-law,
Daughter a mother, daughter-in-law and wife;
Sisters are aunts, brothers are uncles now,
And life is rearranged.
This dance is mastered, ready to enjoy...
So now the time has come to learn the next!

Expected

Darling as yet unborn,

Stirring beneath the family's heart

(Not only mine)

Who are you?

What are you given for?

What will begetting mean

In pain and joy?

Darling as yet unborn,

Hearts stir to know what you are like

(Not just your face.)

We are your near,

Not chosen, but designed:

May we be dear to you

In pain and joy!

For Rachel, May 1999

Taking Bearings on a Promise

Carry? Who will carry? I will!

Carry till your hair is white –

Silver like the Winter hoar-frost –

Sign of vanished might and skill.

I will carry, always carry,

Carry on, and carry through

Loss of senses, independence,

Family, lovers, friends and work.

Leading may not be enough –

Carry I will, like a babe

Through your learning second childhood,

Entrance-ticket at the gates.

If you struggle, still I'll carry –

Hold you closer to my heart –

You are mine, and mine the promise;

Being mine your only part.

Isaiah 46 verses 3-4

Listen to Me, descendants of Jacob, all who are left of My people: I have cared for you since you were conceived, and carried you since you were born. I am your God, and I will sustain you even to your old age, when your hair is white. I have made you and I will carry you; yes, I will carry you Myself, and I will rescue you.

Isaiah 63 verse 9

In his love and in his pity he redeemed them; and he bore them and carried them all the days of old.

Matthew 18 verse 3

Jesus said, "Unless you turn right round, change, and become like little children, you cannot enter the kingdom of heaven."

Coming of Age

Celebrate the coming of age?
Yes, we can celebrate the prospect
Of wrinkles and decline,
Dependency, rheumatics, memory failure,
Peer demise,
Because we see them only as a sign,
The markers of past treasure,
Future hope!
Now we have more to look back on;
More on which to base
Sure choices;
Experience of how our expectations
Have matched reality –
The way things have turned out
When all is said and done.
We know what matters to us when
The chips are down,
And what we can depend on
When all else fails.
As our strength dwindles,
We see another generation rising up
Full of fresh energy and zest.
As we depend perforce, we must
Let go and trust.
Time now to reflect, complete, take stock,
Make sure relationships are sound,
And fix our hope on God
Who is our Rock.

Diary

Why do I write?
To put the pain in focus;
to preach myself a sermon;
to clear my mind and tease out tangled issues;
record amazing ways that things work out.

It's for myself:
and yet the idea of another reader
is not entirely absent.
Perhaps one day (one leisured armchair day?)
I'll turn it into something?

I'd like to have a reader
to share the wonder of God's ways with us,
and then I'd need a record to remind me
how hard the hard days felt, sustained and kept
by hope and trust, now plainly justified.

(One does forget with birth
the labour that precedes,
however long it was.)

Then insights and perceptions
and years of thought and twisting puzzlement,
recorded exercises of my soul
I long to multiply, develop, hone by interchange.
So someone needs to hear.

And yet I'm scared that if I die before
the work of reading, sifting, editing is done,
someone I love will get the wrong idea:
read it, and fail to read between the lines
where most of it's recorded.

But I won't burn my books; it feels too soon
before they are worked through.
I'll trust instead that I can make a will
and leave them in safe hands to do no harm,
and be disposed of rightly.

GOD...

WE'RE DIZZIED BY SIZE,

DAZZLED BY GLORY,

ALARMED BY MYSTERY,

STUMPED BY PARADOX,

SCARED BY TRUTH –

(MAKES MY EYES SMART.)

HOW CAN WE KNOW YOU,

WHEN WE STOP

BEFORE WE START?

Anaesthetic

Adam slept
while you fashioned his bride
from his flesh, from his rib, from his side.

Jesus wept.

EVE

This second Eve

has failed

as failed the first;

but unlike that first Adam

Adam Christ

refused the apple

and embraced the

Cross.

Church?

A place

Where you can face

Your past

And live.

No stone is cast

By fellow glass-house dwellers

Nurtured in light,

And never asked to give

Except by overflow.

A comfort-zone where you can know

Your debts are paid in blood

And weakness understood

And helped.

Integrity the goal –

But on the way

Such succour for the soul!

Dandelion

My friend said
"When I see a dandelion
I let it speak to me."
Bald, pock-marked head,
ruffed with sharp withering fronds,
naked amidst a field of cloth of gold,
what would you say?

"Deep-rooted flowers we.
Decisions
earth-shaking in effect go on in us:
whether to open to the sun or not;
whether to close upon the seed,
and keep fortressed,
or, throwing caution to the winds
(and seeds), court nakedness
and choose to shake the earth
with next year's roots."

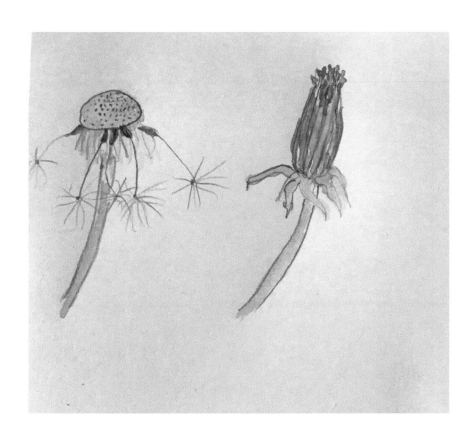

The First Stone...

Was Achan

Of all Israel the only man

Who saw and coveted and
hid

Forbidden things?

Or as the die

Was cast

Did each man shake,

Seeing in his mind's eye

The tent-floor of his heart

And in the funeral pyre

His burning

And in the grave of stone

His own?

Execution

Rather than watching the axe fall

Or the noose jerk to a standstill,

Or life ebb through soldiers' nails,

God decreed capital punishment

(After due course of law)

By stoning.

Not a spectator sport.

Did He assume that men,

Made in His image, though fallen

Would find the act impossible?

Or did He rather know

The worst part of our stain

Was our hypocrisy?

In casting each our stone

We each plead guilty to this charge

Only to be redeemed by

Crucifixion.

Wait

Tense like a bowstring, or taut and twisted like twine,

I wait

For teaching, for light, for a word,

For the joy of His face.

qawah

Still, like the earth for the rain or the babe for a smile,

I lie

In trustful dependence and rest –

He will lift me again.

dum

Peering through mist for a light or a shape or a form

I hope

For rescue, for justice, for life,

For a way in the dark.

yachal

Like a woman in labour, a man under threat of attack,

I writhe,

In suspense, in the anguish of outcome,

The hope against hope.

Chaka

Ready for action, but patient and watching

I'm poised.

Long it may be, but the end is assured –

He will come!

Chil

In italics are the 5 Hebrew words translated 'wait' in the Bible, AV.

Peace & Pain

Peace and pain are not apart.

Peace of heart

Can rest with ache – or even rent

While wresting meaning from event.

How to love with imperfection

Here and elsewhere is the question.

Frown

He disapproved of carryings-on,

dancing, feasts, colour and such-like,

getting merry –

getting married!

One wedding he even turned

wine into water!

Referendum

Misinformation, ignorance abound.

Cross in the box by every 'common man'

Mocks

Choice, substituting chance.

But in each voter's heart

A separate prayer, mighty in its effect –

'Your will be done!'

For peace and justice and for discipline.

So that the utter outcome is of God.

Proverbs 16.33

Marriage

the crucible
where precious metals
are refined, and true amalgams made;
pestle and mortar
combining aromatic healing herbs
for medicine to the world around
(or fragrance);
smooth ointments for life's sores,
and blended spices
to enhance each feast and each
prophetic celebration;
another chance to contemplate
the Eden fruit,
and this time see and choose aright
together;
something not yet complete,
and only to be perfected
under a strong, persistent lifelong
(and much longer)
loving tutelage.

Divorce

Let those whose marriages are Eden-like,

Who never in remotest thought broke faith,

Cast the first stone.

Matthew 19.8 'It was not so from the beginning...'

John 8.7 'Let him who is without sin cast the first stone.'

Dissonance

Teach us how to disagree –

something much more constructive,

organic, dynamic,

than just agreeing to differ –

a quite ecstatic counterpoint of love:

how to be one

and different.

Dialectic

I argued hard against

What showed up in the end

To have been best:

Called to act devil's advocate unconsciously

For God:

Not to oppose his will

Nor yet defend

But introduce into its paradox

The right degree of tension.

And I obeyed.

Phone

When you phone me
I really want to hear
Heart-to-heart,
Not just receiver-to-ear.
Words fall too flat,
And tone is not enough.
But there's an art in that
And that
Is tough

!

Woven

You know my warp, my woof, my twist –
The fabric of my woven being,
Held on a wider loom;
My tension and my slack,
My texture and my feel.
Spun on your wheel
And dyed,
My very yarn is yours.

Psalm 139

Marital Dysrhythmia

Sometimes we tango

at a tangent.

Our minuet's

a minute

out of time.

Our waltz

collides with the walls

(which even a trotting fox could topple).

His quickstep starts

while I am doing a slow

turn.

He holds my hand – I follow – he lets go.

He comes behind to push me into step,

and turns aside instead

to pick up all

that I have dropped.

Now I have

stopped.

I watch him dancing with both hands encumbered.

What is the art?

When can the true dance

start?

YOU

I need **you.**

Not what's left buried under the day's rubble,

Ready for sleep,

But rather you –

Buoyed up by stimulus –

Sharing your outward-look

And gleaning instincts;

Delighting in them with me –

And sharing my inward

Thoughts and joys.

Not you-on-the-shortest-line-from-A-to-B-picking-me-up-in-

passing,

But you in your dearness,

At your best – most thoughtful,

Most compassionate –

I need

You.

I need **you** to work with, yes,

But you to play with, pray with, learn with, dream with too.

Not you-at-a-run-with-never-time-to-stop,

But you to delight with, rest with,

Bless, and be blessed by:

My Darling, I need

You.

If I Stop

Will you come back to look for me?

Linger with me?

Enquiringly?

Or will life whirl you on

Beyond my ken,

My closest kin?

Leave me

Bereft?

Retirement

Work had buried you –

The real You.

Now you can rise again

And look around to view

What life might hold.

You know about the pain

Already. But what about

The gold?

Palm Sunday

'Needs me?'

In what way can that be

Who surely has no unmet need,

No lack?

Perhaps he needs my cheer to join the throng –

My song, my bray?

He needs my back?

I feel his mighty weight,

Nothing so heavy ever felt before!

I shy at flapping cloaks and waving palms,

Panicking till I feel a calming touch

The pressure of his thighs against my sides.

He knows the way an untried colt must feel,

And lets me know which way he'd have me go.

A gentle nudge warns me to skirt a branch,

Step over some child's foot.

I feel his yearning, sorrow amongst cheers.

Towards Jerusalem.

We pass between the gates

And in. The shouting fades.

Tears wet my flanks,

And sobs pulse in my sides.

No-one else notices.

Strip-tease

How you do tease with longing, my Beloved,
undressed, your arms spread wide
in welcoming embrace.
your eyes
filled with the tenderest love
and tears
and yearning.

Why do you not embrace me?
gather me to your heart?
find me and lose me in undying love?

I gaze, amazed, and aching with desire:
your face – is bleeding where the beard is plucked
out by the roots, even around your mouth,
whose kisses linger like the sweetest wine.
Premature age and sorrow line your brow, streaming with sweat;
those darling crows-feet are obscured – or lost for ever.
Vultures brood darkly, doves have fled.
Blood matts your tangled hair.

Pain's ugly vice twists your mouth (the only vice you know)
and scars de-face you – spoil all your handsomeness
to other eyes than mine –
define you, and display your love to me:
they happened in my rescue.

Brutal thongs bind your artist-hands –
touching, expressive, musical hands
fixed like a gamekeeper's lure to a gate –
skewered with masonry nails,
hostage-fixed to wood.

Until our wedding night
(the final d of "finished!")
I cannot feel in flesh the embrace I need.
But oh! the very thought of it
teases my heart to bursting-point with joy!

Desperate Means...

Desperate means to win my love –
dangerous freedom to make dread mistake
without restraint, to leave me uncompelled,
at liberty to make a real response.

Loving

It's like taming a wild shy thing;
It's turning compassion into a womb –
Embracing by letting go;
Gazing with understanding by looking away;
It's winning respect from the headstrong
And trust by absorbing the pain.
It's like
Him.

Hyacinth

Dark, husky bulb.
Outwardly dead,
And kept in darkness.

Life-giving Water
Not even touching
Draws out its roots.

After cold Winter
From shrunken bulb
Fragrance and colour!

Hope and certainty
Fuse!

Cinderella

Kissing a frog

could only ever make

a wooden prince:

but when the Bridegroom chooses

to kiss the girl who sorely needs his love,

a princess comes to life and learns to dance.

Mary

She knew what most men want,

And he did not.

Beams of compassion,

Gentle understanding

And in-love-ness

Streamed from his eyes,

With absolutely no demands.

Total security.

Receiving her touch,

Her hair,

Her perfume as they were given.

Breathing forgiveness.

Love's Brink

To love means pain.

But do not think

When on the brink of love again

That not to love escapes.

To lose what we have loved

Is never loss

Because Love lives in us.

To lose what we have failed to love

Is not the loss it seems,

But bitter pain indeed

Because our door is shut to Love himself

And he without.

So do not reckon

To swerve the pain of love

When next he beckon.

HUG

A hug –

A gesture?

So much more

Between believers –

A sign, icon, symbol,

Yes, even a sacrament

Of unconditional warmth.

xOx

What happens in-between enactments?

Truth fills the place.

Memory and imagination

Speak to the heart

In constant reminder

'You are loved'.

xOx

What you for a brief moment felt

Is real, actual,

Lasting.

Moment by moment

The body remembers

And is comforted.

Climax?

What are they for, these short-lived moments of ecstasy?

Surely not only for these short-lived moments?

As a bud unfolds to a flower

A mustard-seed to a kingdom

Are we making love?

Or is love making us

More eternal, more ephemeral?

Squeezing us through a narrow

Gate

Along a narrow path, hedged high,

Into a wide and sunny plain

Under a wide and shining sky,

Where waits for us ecstasy and communion

Hardly foreshadowed by our greatest bliss?

Is it for this?

Secret Couplets

My secret's a language, but also a need.
My secret's a feeling but also a deed.

My secret's a mystery, but will be revealed.
My secret is wounded, but soon to be healed.

My secret's a whole of which we see part.
My secret is outward, but pierces the heart.

My secret's a symbol, but also a fact.
My secret's a wonder that's ours to enact.

Longing

When, Lord, when?

I sense the edge of glory:

My heart begins to rise in expectation –

Put on her sweetest dress, and standing, wait

In hope of drawing near at last to kiss,

Feeling your love for me.

And then, O then

The gladness seeps away –

Focus is dissipated on externals –

Like petals, bride-clothes droop.

Yet still perhaps joy waits, only deferred?

Patience! Perhaps... perhaps?

But then bent head of waiting

Turns to the bend and shake of disappointment –

The aching surge of tears and longing unfulfilled:

When, Lord, when?

Courtship

What he has done commands my love,

And every day's fresh doing

Shows one whose nature is to love –

Tact, gentleness, respect and passion mixed –

Could I resist such wooing?

Friend

Can I really count you as my Friend?

Always disposed to understand, not judge,

Despite a lifestyle which puts mine to shame?

Delight

Signs of a costly, sacrificial love

Make a wife's heart sing!

She knows that he will give himself for her

And wants to lift her up,

Make her feet dance

And all her footsteps light!

Praise fills her cup!

Affirming ways that she is beautiful

Not to herself but him,

Brims her with gladness –

An orgasm of love and tenderness!

She cannot but respond!

He to Her

Give yourself to me, my Love, total and entire;

Only keep within your heart things that hidden lie,

Lest, with secret hopes and joys, and passion's burning fire

Secret fears and hurts and wrongs all restraint deny.

Only say to me my Love, "I am wholly yours":

Say it with your sweet embrace, and your lips to mine!

Honeyed lips are meant for lips – ears have other laws;

Hush! Let's meet in married bliss, drink unsullied wine!

She to Him

Let me give myself to you, total and entire;

Here's my woman's heart laid bare, gazing through my eyes.

Here are insights, anger, fears, joys and passion's fire:

Make them molten, squeeze them out, in words and smiles and sighs!

But – restrain a part of them – seal my lips with yours

While the vessel still boils full, molten gold and dross,

And you cannot have your Love, sweetness without sores.

Ah! Let's meet in married bliss, and share both crown and cross!

Problem

You tell me the question to ask

before giving the answer.

You never suggest a solution

which in an ideal world would work,

but not in ours.

With you, "heavenly-minded" is a

strictly utilitarian epithet:

"Head-in-the-clouds"

means

"Feet-on-the-ground".

You can find us a way of keeping noses to grindstone

without wearing away our fragrance-perception,

paradox though that be.

You give work when life hangs limp

and rest when tasks press out of mind.

The "how" I leave to you –

or rather look to you to demonstrate

step by small step.

This and That

The fulness of the breast and the roundness of the thigh,

The strength of the sinews and the straightness of the eye,

The sweetness of the smile and the softness of the skin,

The firmness of the mouth and the stubble on the chin,

The dream way of seeing and the gentleness of feel,

The keen way of thinking and the turning on the heel,

The warmth of receiving and the ardour of the gift

The contrast and the merging; the joining and the rift.

Birthright

What is the worth

Of such a document

Right in the midst of life's

Hungers, impatiences, strifes?

Eucharist Whenever

Four Vignettes

'Whenever you eat this bread and drink this cup, you are showing the Lord's death until he comes.' 1 Cor 11.24

Vignette One

A festal celebration.

Heavenly music

Improvised by angels it must be.

Incense rising – and prayer.

Symbolic vestments,

Each piece a message for the eyes –

Colour, glory, sacrifice.

Feast for the senses.

Candles, high-vaulted ceiling,

Beauty everywhere.

Crucifix (remember). And gold

Reflected in the finest sherry-wine.

Light wafers of unleavened bread

Depict sinless perfection, human frailty.

Three readings, the Book treasured and kissed.

The sacred moment when my heart

Focuses its thanksgiving.

'For the heart of the Eternal is most wonderfully kind

– is most wonderfully, wonderfully wonderfully kind.'

(organ improvisation on these lines)

Vignette Two

A few of us, friends,

Brothers and sisters

Here to remember,

And cheer each other on.

We sing a hymn or two.

'Jesus, your blood and righteousness
My beauty is, my glorious dress...'

'Grace and love, like mighty rivers
Flowed unending from above,
And heaven's grace and perfect justice
Kissed a guilty world in love.'

We see the loaf unbroken

Before the empty cross

(For he is here)

And with our own hands break it

And eat, thinking of Jesus.

The blood-red juice

Is poured out as we watch,

(No alcoholic stigmatised or tempted,

For we are one in need and weakness.)

A silver carrier holds the tiny glasses,

Our faces shining back as each one takes.

We drink together.

'Thank-you, Jesus, Thank-you, Jesus,
Thank-you Lord for loving me.'

We love you, Lord!

Vignette Three

Our family is at supper.

First we sing grace, as we so often do:

'We thank you Lord for Jesus Christ,
And for the blood he shed,
We thank you for his risen life,
And for our daily bread.'

Dad has a glass of wine,

Its vermilion reflecting on the table.

Mum drinks water – she can't manage wine.

Shepherd's pie today. Or macaroni cheese.

We chat, sharing our day.

Christ is the unseen Guest at every meal.

The children grow in understanding.

The baby bangs a spoon on her high chair.

We all remember, and are full of joy

Half-understood.

Meal-times are good.

Vignette Four

A solitary cell.

Damp, cold and cheerless.

Here only for the crime

Of loving him.

A mouldy crust my only food today.

Only myself to consecrate that bread,

And make it special.

Water waiting its miracle.

No company but all the saints and angels.

I eat and drink remembering, and worship.

I have no voice to sing,

But whisper hoarsely

'Thank-you my Father.'

'Feast after feast thus comes and passes by
Yet, passing, points to that glad feast above,
Giving sweet foretaste of the festal joy,
The Lamb's great bridal feast of bliss and love.'

Passover

We live within a house whose doorposts gleam

A rusty red,

And all whom that house holds

Are dealt with differently.

Cause and effect are subtly modified

By small unnoticed touches.

Rash, foolish choices find to their surprise

A happy outcome.

Pain holds a meaning.

Even death itself becomes an angel

Permitted as a special messenger:

The poisoned chalice drunk, the Drinker lives

And overshadows.

Grace reigns!

Does this give the impression that God puts aside cause and effect, or allows us to be irresponsible? Does it ignore the hard ways of God? Or is that truly the way God works?

Envy

Nothing mealy-mouthed and colourless

Could make Jews jealous!

Freaked-out on festivals –

A dancing, celebrating people –

(Between such sufferings),

How could a lukewarm mediocrity

Appeal to passion, down-to-earth

And dazzled by the rainbow-glory

Of their Creator God?

Normal Routine

Sudden, unexpected things

Happen regularly!

How can I keep control

When all secure routine –

Every predictability –

Is an illusion?

Even a steady breeze

Turns fluky?

Only skilled trimming of my sails,

And a firm hand over mine

On the tiller

Will carve a way

Through restless waters

To a safe shore.

Departure Lounge

I thought of jets, and panicked.

All that squeezing and twisting of time

To and fro!

And yet in sleep each night encapsulated

We yield ourselves, and breathing

To and fro,

Our dreams warp time, and strangely bring together

Our loves and hates, and our forgotten selves.

PLAY

'If we learn to work by playing,

how can we learn to play

if we've forgotten?'

Ephemeral

Everything exists, like manna

On a daily basis.

Flowers and birds know it.

Each morning

A new today –

All possessions leased,

And all gifts

Yielded up in sleep.

We are intended

To recognise

That we have lost

Control

(Or never had it

Except by delegation).

Even night-shifters nod or blink –

Sometimes for nanoseconds

Night-watchmen doze.

The local church

Is defined on a daily basis

As leaders fall asleep

And emails are shut down.

The church suffers

A discontinuous break –

Sleeps and is recreated –

Reconstituted

Reappointed for today's task.

Meantime God is in charge –

That Great Shepherd –

By hook or by crook

Holding all things together

World without end.

Nazareth Whispers

He's the living image of his mother!

The way he looks at you!

That searching, questioning gaze,

And then a gentle smile

As if he understood your very thoughts.

He sometimes has the look of his Grandpa too

(Upon the distaff side you know

For – tell it not in Gath –

He was the aftermath

Of an unfortunate affair.)

Such a nicely brought up girl too –

You wouldn't have thought it of her –

And far from hanging her head in shame

She seemed to walk on air

Once Joseph had taken her on.

They went away for the event itself

At census time, year before last.

Came back last week, with him

Just two years old and into everything!

His dad (so to say) gave him his own little tool set

And showed him how to use it.

You'd think he was born to carpentry –

Strokes the wood with the grain

And turns it in his hand,

Copies every movement Joseph makes

Then runs back to his mum to show her.

Sometimes he looks at the sky calling **Abba**,

As if he'd find him there.

Whatever does he mean?

Currency

Money, time and energy are interchangeable currencies.
Overdraft on one account can be replaced by drawing on another.
Exhaust all three, and plain insolvency
Ensues...
– An undesirable state of affairs!

Money, time, and energy
Should be
(in an ideal world)
Fully interchangeable currency.
We work towards it.

Take Care

'Take care', she said.

What happens if – just for one moment –
I forget?

I'd rather hear 'Farewell', or better far, 'Goodbye', and
walk secure
In God my Father's care.

Miser

If time is money,

then love of time

is the root of all evil.

Conversely...

A generous inner eye

when budgeting our time

could be the root of all good...

Pharisee

I hate that pharisee

into whose house I sometimes come invited

and dine;

for his is not another's house

but mine.

Overdraft

Each failing and shortcoming

(Debit on life's account)

Plunges me in the Red.

And I will never shed

My fully fluctuating

Overdraft.

Job

The right tool for the right task at the right time.

Waste

Waste is not pouring out for love,

but hoarding close for fear...

Affliction

Many-stranded is affliction's rope
To bind, or draw, or lift:
What God intends is complex, intertwined.
Correction (need enough for every day
To turn my self-ward bias);
Testing of strength (and weakness);
A demonstration to the powers that be
(Job-like) that God's own children live by love;
Sharing Christ's sufferings (strange mystery –
Those sufferings were for me).
So I will wait with patient, aching heart
And twisted longings, taut, intense and strained,
For God to speak, but with a Father's tone.
Simply I'll wait, twisting expectancy
Out of despair; writhing in birth-pangs;
For it is the Lord
Who waits
for me.

Tidesturn

The moment of change has no fanfare:

Almost imperceptibly

The tide turns in deep water

Marked by hardly a quiver

The whole direction changes

Charted by not so much as a damp sinking line on the sand,

And by this turn initiates

The rush and surge and tumble

Of the incoming water:

A strength to wash away what stood,

Wipe clean and rearrange a whole wide shore.

Tides

I need the ebb and flow – both flow and ebb –

The ebb which opens up new depths to light –

The flow which reaches heights as yet untouched,

And licks the feet of rocks, and washes silt.

For him, life is aflow from day to day,

And only ebbs with each wave's undertow.

For me, the impact of each breaking wave

On shifting shingle is not flow enough.

You who made night and day and season's change,

Will you in love coordinate our seas?

Our times are in your hands – so too our tides.

Or else I'll long to be a moon to him,

And charm his tides in unison with mine.

No, rather let him only know the ebb

Of your bright sun's evaporating power

Drawing him up, despite the unrelenting flood and flow of
  life.

Small Boat in a Wide Sea

When tides are strong, and strength for rowing fails,

There is a heavenly Wind to fill our sails;

A gentle prompting of our tiller hand

To keep us safe on course, and soon to land.

Low Tide

Low tide and stillness. All has ebbed –

Strength, purpose, health, ideas and joy.

Friends have receded.

Shore is a featureless expanse,

With no wind-movement on the sea.

My boat lies moored, off-balance, high and dry.

I need not think

That there will never come again a flow –

For this is tide and mighty sea,

Not sink,

And One who made the oceans, moon and me

Rules!

Black and White

To see things in black and white

Is to count as visually impaired,

For light surely reveals not only shades of grey

But colours – subtle differences of hue

Allowing a full assessment of what we look upon.

And yet... to limit eyes to black and white

Defines some tones and shades

Which otherwise we'd miss,

And in a sense sharpens our sight.

Monochrome

Why can a photograph in black and white
Be sometimes more evocative by far
Than one in glorious colour? Could it be
That one dimension less can somehow point
To one dimension more?

And that distraction which depression brings,
With over-sensitiveness and self-doubt –
Could it be like a lens held close to life
Whose blurring edges fade out all one world
To fade in all another?

These shuttings-down, restrictions, blurrings, frames,
Which ache the spirit's eyes and numb the heart
With unnamed hopeless longings – could they be
God's way of focussing beyond myself
Into relief on Him?

Depths

We who have plumbed our depths are more secure –

Our enemies no more in ambush lie:

No more the cracking twig alarms our hearts

With large imaginings of hidden fear;

We know their faces – see them line by line.

Like portrait painters we have well defined

Their ugliness and weakness, and have found

A human face where goodness lurks in bad.

We can discern a Father's love and care

In stress, and doubled trouble, and distress.

We know His sure intent to make us whole,

That, deeply calm and knowing His peace unknown,

We can withstand, and stand with arms outstretched

To those who blithely walk into their trap,

Or, still alarmed, creep limping on through life.

I'd rather far go through my valley now

And sing when prison comes, or death, or doom,

Than go unknowing till dereliction strikes.

NARROW WAY

How can I do what you command, my Lord?

("Why do you call me 'Lord'?")

How can I love her whom my soul detests?

What use is love through gritted teeth, I ask,

With hatred underneath?

I want to follow you, but loving her

Is far too dear a price for me to pay.

What's that you say?

Just give you leave to love her in your way?

Can I agree?

Stone

Hard as stone.
Impenetrable, dense.
What it encloses
Hides secure,
Perceived only by
A gifted eye
Insight, skill
A will.

Sentient Stone

If stone could feel, what would it say when hand-worked by a

Master Mason?

Michelangelo's sculpture, Atlas

Stonemason

They say a master mason liberates

from rough-hewn stone what his great skill imagines.

'Leave me alone' my rough-hewn block implores.

'Chisel and mallet hurt!'

What did I mean by 'me'? An entity still living in

the inner eye of God?

'Would that I never was and never may be'! Is that indeed

my deepest heartfelt wish?

Home's Porch

"I'm an outliver" she said
In heaven's anteroom,
Specially prepared
And pre-occupied
So never lonely.
Memory fails, so
Breathtaking, breath-holding
Anticipation
Gets more and more
Vital
!

Present

It is a gift to live now
focussing on the moment
of outer scene, not inner only:
not yesterday, tomorrow or the possible,
but choosing to honour, weight with present notice
faces and clouds and trees,
and recognise their meaning,
knowing I am,
and loving.

Both these poems were written about my mother in November 1990

Rankle

Forgiveness is hard, because of pain.

Pain rankles, re-echoes, stabs,

Changes my feelings, not for a finite time (say, 7 years)

But for a life. It sources all my tears;

Doesn't allow forgetting; grabs

My throat again, again;

Only ever allows a comma in the long sentence of suffering.

Forgiveness is excusing, letting off the hook.

Justice cries out: wrong must be recognised, atoned,

Punished, exact its penance.

That is, until I see myself, in tortured dance,

Wriggling on that self-same cunning hook;

And then implore, implore release with opened, weeping eyes.

But how to feel my weakness, without the self-same trial?

How can I know how much it all depends

Upon the hand I'm dealt?

How would I be if I had walked that mile,

That tortured mile, in someone else's shoes,

With someone else's troubles, limps and burdens?

In their furnace, would I really melt?

What might I do, and how lash out in pain,

Inflicting hurt? Unstoppable and irremediable,

Ruining another's life?

How I would crave forgiveness! And do, for the bent is there.

Can I believe the alchemy of bringing good from evil?

Know that it really happens, that great marvel,

Redemption?

Here lies the test of faith, and I must stand!

Ne méprise pas...

Never despise

the path that winds,

the steepness

and the heavy boots.

Humble self-mastery

is won no other way

than step

by step.

Hard saying

He drives his sheep out

(to the haunt of wolves?)

but goes before them.

For Wind drove him out once into the wild,

(deserted?) plagued by hungry predators,

and only after forty days of raging

turbulence

(not still waters)

and arid wastes

(not wasted, but not green)

did angels minister.

Dark Valley

Cudgel and crook, cudgel and crook

I trudge in the comfort of cudgel and crook.

Home

Where is home?
It's where I can relax and be myself
Knowing I am fully understood
And loved beyond limits.
It is a place of safety and protection –
A place of welcome, rest, refreshment,
Of smiles and joy and comfort.

Where is this ideal home?

My Father's house, none other;
And I am often homesick.

Restoration

Rest, and reflect, beside the given still waters.
Store up the sense of cherishing He gives.
Rate pauses highly – shun for a while the race.
Wait till your step is sprightly once again
Before you put your foot upon the bridge
That takes you back to service and employ.
Take time to savour joy.

Psalm 23

None of my needs shall be unmet

Not even need of need

(Of hunger, thirst, fatigue)

To drive me to the Source of all supply.

Quis custodiet ipsos custodes?

Who guards the guards?

Manages managers?

Fathers fathers?

Rules the King?

Who takes care of caretakers?

Presides over the President?

Doctors physicians?

Judges judges?

The Prime Mover!

Proactive First Cause!

Underived Love!

Maker Unmade!

Where does the buck stop?

Here!

David

The suit of armour was a size too large –

rigid, unhinged except at joints which didn't match his own;

put on him with the very best intentions –

supposed to help him fight on their behalf

along accustomed lines,

but ponderous and ungainly, an encumbrance –

heavy mud-anchor,

rooting him

to the

spot.

He had to throw it off, not to abandon fight,

but face it in a vulnerable way,

with skills God gave him, trained by God alone

(choosing the right smooth word to hit the mark,

his bear and lion searisks and unforgiving crofting land)

distinctive, individual and natural,

effective for the kingdom,

killing giants.

for David Middlemiss

Risky Thinking

Are there some paths of thought I dare not follow
Because they could lead to a hanging edge
Where, brink-perched, I might plummet to the rocks
Of black despair – or slip with straying foot
Into the sliding, sucking, swallowing mud?

Yet some most risky wanderings lead to light,
And, never dared, all would be darkness still.

When from the tunnel of perplexity
I sought a way, in groping desperation,
All chinks were dangerous and hid, I knew,
Rock-falls and floods and risk of long starvation.

Yet I emerged, and lived. So now I dare
To set my testing foot upon those paths
Of thought, too narrow
Ever
To turn back.

Broad is the way, and not a narrow track
That leads to death. And I walk not alone.

Angst

When I saw how big and bad the world

(protective roofing Hand removed for a moment to allow a
glimpse)

I feared with mortal terror.

But if the Living God is made of love,

and formed entire the cosmos intricate –

matter itself from nothing but a charge of super-dynamism,

and we from atom dust –

why, then I feared no more, relaxed, and live by trust.

The World...

The world is beautiful –

Achingly lovely,

Surprising in grandeur,

Colour and detail.

The world is ugly,

Blistering hideous,

Searing, mangling,

Shattering.

We're made, like God

With feelings,

Preoccupying, intense

Defining.

Beauty will last for ever,

Ugliness vanish in a flash –

Beauty for ash,

Gladness for tears.

Remade.

Crystal Moon

Clear as water, curved as outer space,

The spiral form of life,

Marking months and tides,

Reflecting waves – and gardens,

A paradox of point and arc,

Ethereal and solid,

Tactile, smooth and grained,

She shines, and shining lights,

Illuminating thought.

Overhill

Over the hill,

So heart-constricting steep,

So rending rugged,

There lies a valley

Sweet, and bathed in sun.

So many weary footsteps lead that way,

That looking back I faint.

But looking on,

I know that that sweet place will soon be won.

Sculpture

Moon on a midnight sea

a mighty calm

waxed water shaped by an unseen power

fragmented droplets massed into unity

heavy with meaning

too deep for waves

too strong for agitation

bent

turned

drawn

raised

and held in tension

curved

funnelled

like the universe itself

reflecting a moment

and

beyond all time

dark shining

moving stillness

ebb and flow

all one

immensity

gazed on with bated breath...

On seeing a black marble sculpture entitled 'Moon on a Midnight Sea' by Shelley Robzen

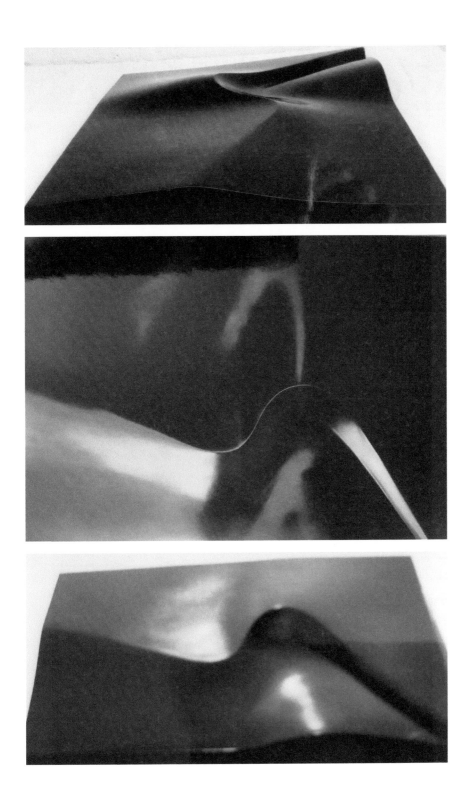

Upwardly Mobile beyond Blue

Twin helix of three-coloured sails
cut out of sheeted steel,
strung like an eastern wind-chime,
each triangle fragmentary,
distinct, a pointed
statement...

Shining, poised, delicate,
related, but free to be itself,
hard steel bent in soft bunting curves,
(rose, indigo, magenta, copper, gold)
catching the light, but never capturing,
mirroring turret bars
but not imprisoned...

Up up
spiralling, lifting,
waiting the gentlest eddy,
(guarded from whirlwinds by the encircling tower),
the lightest breath to play the colours,
turn and tune the
changes...
Kaleidoscope
held in a web of threads,
limited by a frame from rising to the blue,
beyond breath,
beyond achievement,
I view this trinity as if myself,
standing galleried beside its maker,
and reflect...

On viewing a mobile sculpture ('Blue Beyond')
beside the sculptress, Diane Maclean.

In Nancy's Church

There's beguiling light through the unbarred prison window;
I long to dance, but a panther stalks my heels;
The water's edge calls "come" but my skirt's too heavy;
How can I love when I have no arms to embrace?
I cock my head like a bird alert and listening –
Ecstatic music teases my longing ears.

I'm like a swimmer checked in the act of diving;
I'm like a boat on the slipway almost launched;
I can't get out of the house I know is burning
I can't get in to the house that's cool and green;
My kitchens past are chequered with criss-cross longings –
Rigid-roofed when I long to fly to the stars.

I climb a spiral to view the world around me;
I feel screwed-up when I glimpse the world within;
I'm a lonely cargo set on a long voyage;
I'm a child held safe in a world too big to know;
My senses sing in a wealth of shape and colour;
My spirit aches to move in a dance of joy.

I want to own the passing flash of the diamond;

I want to catch the fleeting breath of the wind;

I want to change with the whirl and surge of oceans;

I want to rest in the comfort of a home.

I know myself as a maze of contradictions –

I let myself be known by amazing Love.

This poem was written when staying in an
American friend's house which was a converted
Church filled with an amazing variety of
pictures and objets d'art.

Helix

My mind is dark

and seething

with strange shapes.

Chaos and darkness

joined

another time

in genesis.

Awaits my seething, incoordinate mass

the brooding Dove, the quickening Breath,

to sweep

and whirl the acid molecules

to helices of life.

Spiral staircase at Girton College

Fearmonger

He's a fear-merchant:

give him any raw terror

(even timidity or insecurity)

add a dash of imagination

and he'll do a reversed alchemy job,

turning the gold of trust and affection

with a lurid flash

into sour cinders –

the ordinary common stuff

of quarrels, suspicion,

misunderstandings, mistakes

misrepresentations –

everything that misses the mark

and lies *askew.*

Truth is his enemy,

real communication his downfall,

trust his ruin.

Imagination mixed with these

makes an electrolytic restoration

(gradual, steady, layer by layer)

to burnished glory.

Enemy

He crept in front, ambushed, attacked and fled,

Too strong, too swift for me.

Havoc he left behind, and pain and tears,

And crippling fears.

Psalm 18

Fowler Foiled

Shew me the loophole in the snare,

the catch entrapped in ice,

the secret spring in winter

unlocking frozen vice.

And can you tell me truly where

the setting's on map?

so I can find the double bind

and turning round, unwrap?

Lucifer can't escape his name –

could noose be for lasso

so God can hold and brand and own –

Bring light and let me go?

Battles at Easter-time

Good Friday and its prelude are their chance.

They can mock and scoff and jeer,

Blaspheme and hate with practised ease.

With press-ganged, programmed victims

They can re-enact scourging, lynching,

Crucifixion and betrayal.

All these are Satan's stock in trade.

But Easter they can never show—

Life, resurrection, cleansing, love,

These are God's only.

Look up! Christ is risen!

Jesus is with us!

In captive-liberating power,

He reigns!

Neither death, nor life, nor angels, nor principalities, nor powers,

Nor things present nor things to come, nor height nor depth, nor
any other creature,

Shall be able to separate us from the love of God, which is in
Christ Jesus our Lord.

Romans 8.38-39

Chrysalis

What is this cell – this paralysed existence?
Cramped by self-woven bonds no strength in me can
break,
useless, and large, and cumbersome and tired,
I lie enclosed, and dark and quite alone.

Had I not known sweet life, and shared contentment,
(or, more, communal dangers faced in mutual care ,
my caterpillar legs scuttering away)
then I might close my eyes where no sun is,
and die unanguished. But so dimly, now
I sense that this is not my fated end.

Is it then punishment, so well-deserved,
a prison for the spirit that rebelled,
and would not be confined by gentler means?
Alas, that must be it.
Writhing I spin my bonds
in deep, unmitigated darkness.
Then lie spent,
And cease, all form dissolved.

My first death past, sun-warmth bestirs my sleep,
cracks the dry shell of my self-made cocoon.
I squeeze out trembling, into the leaf-green light
of life unchanged, but shimmering for me
with an undreamed potential.
Brightness dazzles my loneliness.

Crumpled
and foot by foot
I creep,
uncertain,
up the confusing stems,
wondering to be free.

And as I gaze, amazed,
there spreads above, and wing-to-wing
with me
a fluttering veil of myriad butterflies
exulting on the breeze and in the light
of shifting rainbow beauty.

Can one so long-compressed and limited
be liberated undeservingly,
spread radiant wings,
burst into colour, flight and ecstasy?

Only this happening as I died and live
Answers unquestionably
"Yes, o yes!"

My Friend Mary

(or "No Pat Answer")

My friend Mary idled when she ironed,

Cogitated while she cooked,

Danced while she dusted,

Debated inwardly as she drove the kids to school,

She told me with a smile.

(She doesn't work.)

But me, my only reflections
are traffic-lights on a rainy road
as I race to the office
no idling no punctuation-marks all high-power
high-speed high-pressure Life
in the fast lane
in the real world.

I pay Pat to do for me the jobs

which might waste time or thought,

(or space for wondering?)

She shops, cooks, cleans,

and wipes the children's noses.

I'm her Consultant/Manager:

I pay her more than most.

Yet sometimes as I choose the shortest route

and hesitate a moment at the lights,

unsettling flickering thoughts beset my mind:

has my friend Mary found the better part?

Or even Pat who is my employee?

And do I have a choice?

Chess Question

Does God play chess?

And if He does,

will He win

against the world's

Grand Master?

Mirror

Precious as silver

(for silver he was sold)

I am in Him

and one day shall be gold.

I won't forget

my image mirrored there,

of which He counts

and values every hair.

Robin

I sing in ice and frost and snow,

I sing in bitter cold;

I sing because of what I know

Before the buds unfold.

This exquisite painting by wildlife artist
Pollyanna Pickering sparked off a poem.

"I wish I had a faith like yours..."

You ask for a faith like mine;

I ask

For Someone equal to the task

Of rescue.

We both stand on a wall

Too high to jump off

Poised perilously, waiting for a

Fall.

What child

Would leap into the arms

Of someone kind but feeble?

Or throw itself unfearing

Into the strong embrace of someone bad,

Malign, unloving, mad or wild?

How can we know the nature

Of our offered Catcher?

My evidence lies in a Name

Historic Leaper

Reaper and Gatherer

Who threw himself into those arms

On my behalf, and lives,

And opens wide his arms in turn

For me.

Would I...?

Would I

Have shouted 'Crucify!'

Would my voice swell that cry?

Would I have said

'His blood be on my head

And on my children's?'

Yet if I had called out that dreadful curse,

In God's amazing love He made it worse

to justify myself (or try) as Pilate did,

and made His blood the greatest of salvations

with which to bless the coming generations.

'Crucify!' was the only way to save us.

His blood on us (and on our children)

the only way to blessing.

Poem written after singing the St Matthew Passion.

Vision

Though the light

Dazzles,

Though what it shows

Scares,

I want to see.

Salve

To solve my blindness –

Sting

Me into action –

Shock

Me into reality.

Two Ways of Working

The Psychoanalyst

The bud lay tardy closed – his diagnosis –
Perhaps worm-eaten at the heart?
Holding it firm, he crushed its tender form
Resolving to expose its hidden core
For phototherapy.
He stripped the sepals from its outer layer,
Surgically incised fused petal-bases
And grasping the tips between a hardened thumb
And index-finger (quite indicative)
Tore each sap-oozing indeterminate petal
Till the flower was open
And the heart lay
Bare.

The noonday sun in desiccating power
Shone bright and shrivelled it.

The Counsellor

The One who formed the bud
Saw and defined her future with his gaze;
Shined on her with his love long day by day;
Nurtured her with his gentle showers and dews;
Watched while she turned her being
All to him,
Grew, and unlocked her sepals,
Unfurled her petals,
Day after day more rich in vivid colour,
Till all her heart lay
Open.

Then with his smile he warmed her to the core
And brought to fullness all her hidden seed.

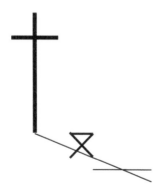

Treasure Hunt Clue

Advent astrologers were led to see

Casting its shadow on the Babe – a tree.

There conflict starts, and also has its end:

Our heavenly Enemy becomes our Friend!

Advent 99

What if...

the millennium bug never bites;

you never need to turn off the Christmas tree lights

(they are simply extinguished by eclipse);

the tree stays decorated, heralding star atop;

holly and ivy deck the halls for Him,

and it turns out to be the definitive

Advent?

What if...

the dome collapses, and plans fail;

a white Christmas is a dream, only a dream,

for now is the time when sleepers wake;

those who expect Him go out with their lamps,

soon to be quite redundant in the Light?

Can we reflect that any minute now might be

The Advent?

Written before 2000

Advent

Ready?

Too soon?

Advent marks the season of

Preparation!

Outside – trees and cards.

Inside – reincarnation.

Every day and

Upwards our eyes lift.

Ready and

Coming!

Incarnation

α α α

Not more abstract, abstruse and

esoteric – a paradigm

appealing to a few initiates

and otherwise incomprehensible

apart from lengthy footnotes;

But clear, earthed, everyday,

sharp, unexpected,

appealing to all ordinary folk;

applicable in concrete ways,

explained by a gasp of insight!

Yet as each single year is named from This,

and the millenia,

surely he would have spoken by a star

in astronomical complexity

had there been even only one

wise man?

Ω Ω Ω

Christmas at Greatham Manor

Not today more than anyday,

Not now more than anytime

We festival your birth

And dance for very joy that you are come.

Knowing neither the day nor hour,

Nor which we celebrate –

Your past or future coming –

We joy you in our hearts.

And all this wealth of colour, music, light,

Family love, exciting expectation,

Breathtaking starlit stillness

All waits to welcome you.

Even so come, Lord Jesus!

Christmas Cactus

Beauty and pain.

Mary, a baby,

Thorns and a cross;

How then it may be

From his loss

Our gain?

Xmas

This Winter feast of mammonmas

I hate!

I will not celebrate

the access of this god!

Tricked out in finery

which costs a bomb,

decked with sham gold and silver

glitter and tinsel garlands;

lashings of lavish gifts

and suicidal debt;

quarrels and family rifts;

queues endlessly;

a feast of migraine and debauchery

(French names to distance them from us)

cake and mince pies and booze

(millennia from bread and wine)

crude office jokes and hollow jollity

not joy.

Can these two celebrations ever mix?

Hawk

They raised him to a golden dais, miles

above the peoples' sorrows and their smiles.
They poured perfumed oblations on his feet
hoping to make his thirst for praise replete.
He loosed the falcon tethered to his wrist.
It gave the day a strange symbolic twist
to see it stoop and lift its struggling prey.
Merciless day.

Dove

They buried him beneath the water, one

With all atrocities the world had done.

One with their inappropriate smiles, and
    tears

Too scanty to express their griefs and
    fears.

He was raised up, and on him from above

Was loosed the surest sign of peace and love

That ever came upon the human race.

O day of grace!

Onion

'There lives the dearest freshness deep down things...'

Gerard Manley Hopkins

Le Gardien

A l'entrée du parc,

C'est le dignitaire de service:

Costume mi-saison – les nuits sont fraîches –

Laissant deviner la puissante carrure,

Les membres vigoureux,

Les mains écarquillées

Avec, au bout des doigts,

Ce frisson de verdure qui ne trompe pas.

A l'entrée du parc,

Il a baissé la garde :

Mais oui, c'est le printemps !

HJ
Mai 2020

Seed... Sapling... Sycamore

First wings and flight – a place to rest.

Why did the wind blow so today?

Rootlets exploring, wriggling between the crumbs of earth

in search of moisture, nourishment and anchor.

Shoot, tender, tentative, pliable, yellowish-green

subject to light and warmth – and weather.

it can be forced to fix in one direction,

but unstaked it will bend and turn and veer,

reaching for what it needs, for what is good;

and even when it reaches sapling-strength,

(bark thickening, roots established, branches formed)

all can be changed.

A neighbour is cut down,

sunshine let in,

excessive growth lopped off,

maximum health achieved,

and freedom to re-fruit

with wings again.

Thoughts about how far we are hard-wired, and how much free to change and be changed.

Storm

Batten down the hatches!

Make the fittings fast!

Drop the sail –

It's blowing a gale –

She risks a broken mast!

Batten down the hatches!

Turn her head-to-wind!

Then she can ride

The wind and tide

Till times are less unkind.

Batten down the hatches

Against the sea and rain!

Now she can last

Till storm is past

And she sets course again.

Winter

O time of change and transformation,

O valley where I walk beset,

O Winter's cold which presages

Another Summer's coming – yet

I shrink from you.

I shrink from all the letting go

Of things familiar and secure –

Cup, hands, heart, empty and upheld

For unimagined blessings – sure

But hidden still.

Yes, hid, and sometimes doubted in

The chill which is the mood of death:

Breathed in by Him who is my life

I wait for His restoring breath

And bow my head.

Immaterial

Yes, we shall meet again,

but when

or where

is either here or there.

Ars Longa – A Reflection

Her eyes question, probe, imagine:

Does she look out from some kind of disguise –

A western purdah, engendering awkward

thoughts

about identity? Or do those eyes

transform her isolation into community?

Is this the healing art?

In this late season (vita brevis est)

Persona clings, a uniform of shrewdness

Learned from experience –

prognosis from frequent diagnosis,

now differently applied.

Could I mistake such probing for a threat?

The eyes meet mine, direct and personal,

Despite the anonymity of mask.

What questions do I ask?

Portrait

Deep to the skin life's sorrows lie

In musculature and in eye.

The face displays without intent

A mind by contradictions rent.

No black and white distinction here

Only an unshed tear.

Impossible Prayer

I want to speak to THAT person there,

On the other side of the world,

In a tiny village, out in the Styx.

I want to see and hear them NOW,

Wherever they are!

Granted!

If man can do that,

What can God not do?

Empty Chair

Come, tell your sadness to the empty chair,

Once burdened with the weight of that lost form.

Come, tell your anger to the empty chair,

Batter its wood with wrath and hear reply.

Come, tell your longings to the empty chair,

Their unfulfillment and their trailing hope.

Come, find the chair no empty passive place,

But peopled with incarnate deity,

With form, reply and hope.

How?

The farmer wished to see things set to rights. He fenced the cattle off,
then turned his brown-britched back towards the cow, and started digging
round to prune the roots.
The cow made hay, and pushed aside the fence to graze the lush green grass.
I don't know how I can think up a good defence against a cow when someone's
back is turned.
Meantime the blackbird chaunteth merrily atop the stately monkey puzzle tree.

My Friend

Have you stopped to puzzle,

Muse, ponder and tease out

Life's twists and turns?

Have you discerned

The richness of the pattern?

Then go on,

Wresting meaning from event,

Cudgel and crook your strength

And breast the length.

BV - #0035 - 301020 - C26 - 234/156/8 - PB - 9781914002007 - Gloss Lamination